V $4

The Little Book of Humorous Quotes

The Little Book of Humorous Quotes is available at special discounts
when purchased in quantities for educational use, fund-raising or
sales promotions. Special editions or book excerpts can also be
created. For more information, please contact:
inspire@littlequotebooks.com.

ISBN-10: 0578086433
EAN-13: 9780578086439
LCCN: 2011930703

www.littlequotebooks.com

The Little Book of Humorous Quotes

Edited by Malcolm Kushner

Contents

Thank You

This book wouldn't exist without the help and encouragement of many people. First and foremost was publisher Kathleen Welton who had the idea for the book and asked me to compile it. Kudos also to Christine Griger, Sam Kushner, Deborah DeCuir, Heather Tamarkin, Amy Tamarkin, Justin Herzfeld and Elizabeth Woodge Stover — they know why. Or maybe they don't.

You can quote me on that.

Introduction

This is a collection of 365 humorous quotes — a quote to use as inspiration for each day of the year. Quotes have been selected to cover a dozen topics. They are arranged for easy access as follows:

* Modern Life
* On the Job
* Rules to Live By
* The Laugh's On Me
* It's Like
* Hearts On Fire
* Friends and Family
* You Talking to Me?
* Defining Moments
* Excellent Observations
* We the People
* As the Years Go By

You'll also notice that months and topics have been matched where appropriate. For example, "The Laugh's On Me" resides in April, which is national humor month. "We the People" is in November, which is the month when elections are held. And "As the Years Go By" is at the end — because the years go by and this is nearly the end of this book. In addition, the quotes are arranged by sub-topics within each topic so that they read like a monologue whenever possible. This is designed to add an extra dimension of humor to quotes that are already individually amusing.

Some of the quotes have been collected by me over the years. Others were researched and selected specifically for this book. My goal has been to bring some laughter into your life when you open these pages. Although everyone disagrees about what's "funny," I hope you'll find that these quotes are at least interesting and entertaining. And if reading them makes milk come out of your nose as you double over and snort — well, that's even better.

Keep laughing!

Malcolm Kushner
September 2011

Modern Life

Everybody wants to help save the earth, but nobody wants to help mom do the dishes.

~P.J. O'Rourke

You know there is a problem with the education system when you realize that out of the 3 R's only one begins with an R.

~Dennis Miller

It's easy to identify people who can't count to ten. They're in front of you in the supermarket express lane.

~June Henderson

Only two things are infinite — the universe and human stupidity and I'm not sure about the former.

~Albert Einstein

Personally, I'm waiting for caller IQ.

~Sandra Bernhard

∽

I wish there was a knob on the TV so you could turn up
the intelligence. They got one marked brightness, but it
don't work.

~Gallagher

∽

Men don't care what's on TV. They only care what else is
on TV.

~Jerry Seinfeld

∽

Computer dating is fine, if you're a computer.

~Rita Mae Brown

∽

For a list of all the ways technology has failed to improve the
quality of life, please press 3.

~Alice Kahn

∽

If you're going through hell, keep going.

~Winston Churchill

∽

When science finally locates the center of the universe, some people will be surprised to learn they're not it.

~Bernard Bailey

∽

Know thyself — but don't tell anyone.

~H.F. Henrichs

∽

I am as frustrated with society as a pyromaniac in a petrified forest.

~A. Whitney Brown

∽

The soup is never hot enough if the waiter can keep his thumb in it.

~William Collier

∽

Some say the glass is half empty, some say the glass is half full, I say, are you going to drink that?

~Lisa Claymen

∽

Red meat is not bad for you. Now blue-green meat, that's bad for you!

~Tommy Smothers

∽

I went to the 30th reunion of my preschool. I didn't want to go, because I've put on like a hundred pounds.

~Wendy Liebman

∽

To learn that all I really need to know I learned in kindergarten, I needed to go to grad school.

~John Alejandro King

∽

Every book is a children's book if the kid can read!

~Mitch Hedberg

∽

Although I can accept talking scarecrows, lions and great wizards of emerald cities, I find it hard to believe there is no paperwork involved when your house lands on a witch.

~Dave James

∽

Once you can accept the universe as being something expanding into an infinite nothing which is something, wearing stripes with plaid is easy.

~Albert Einstein

∽

I think one reason they call them "Relaxed Fit" jeans is that "Ass The Size of Texas" jeans would not sell very well.

~Jim Rosenberg

∽

Guys I've been meeting have the worst pickup lines. Like, "Hey, what's your friend's name?"

~Melanie Reno

∽

Reality is the leading cause of stress among those in touch with it.

~Lily Tomlin

∽

You can't have everything. Where would you put it?

~Steven Wright

∽

If it's free, it's advice; if you pay for it, it's counseling; if you can use either one, it's a miracle.

~Jack Adams

∽

To err is dysfunctional, to forgive co-dependent.

~Berton Averre

∽

When you are smashing monuments, save the pedestals —
they always come in handy.

~Stanislaw J. Lec

∾

A commentary on the times is that the word "honesty" is now
preceded by "old-fashioned."

~Larry Wolters

∾

There is never enough time, unless you're serving it.

~Malcolm Forbes

∾

The fat lady hasn't started to sing yet,
but she has a mic in her hand.

~Ian Holloway

On the Job

The brain is a wonderful organ. It starts working the moment
you get up in the morning and does not stop until
you get into the office.

~Robert Frost

A bad day at work is better than a good day in hell.

~Scott Johnson

One of the symptoms of an approaching nervous breakdown is
the belief that one's work is terribly important.

~Bertrand Russell

Hard work never killed anybody, but why take a chance?

~Edgar Bergen

If hard work is the key to success, most people would rather pick the lock.

~Claude McDonald

∽

When a man tells you that he got rich through hard work, ask him: "Whose?"

~Don Marquis

∽

All I've ever wanted was an honest week's pay for an honest day's work.

~Steve Martin

∽

I always arrive late at the office, but I make up for it by leaving early.

~Charles Lamb

∽

I like work: it fascinates me. I can sit and look at it for hours.

~Jerome K. Jerome

∽

It's amazing how long it takes to complete something you're not working on.

~R.D. Clyde

∽

I love working for myself; it's so empowering. Except when I call in sick. I always know when I'm lying.

~Rita Rudner

∽

I don't want to achieve immortality through my work... I want to achieve through not dying.

~Woody Allen

∽

You moon the wrong person at an office party and suddenly you're not "professional" any more.

~Jeff Foxworthy

∽

If you don't believe in the resurrection of the dead, look at any office at quitting time.

~Robert Townsend

∽

I often feel like the director of a cemetery. I have a lot of people under me, but nobody listens!

~General John Gavin

∽

The key to being a good manager is keeping the people who hate me away from those who are still undecided.

~Casey Stengel

∽

Most of what we call management consists of making it difficult for people to get their jobs done.

~Peter Drucker

෬

Lots of folks confuse destiny with bad management.

~Kin Hubbard

෬

The higher a monkey climbs, the more you see of its behind.

~Joseph Stilwell

෬

Informed decision-making comes from a long tradition of guessing and then blaming others for inadequate results.

~Scott Adams

෬

After the ship has sunk, a consultant knows how it might have been saved.

~Newt Hielscher

෬

Blinding speed can compensate for a lot of deficiencies.

~David Nichols

෬

It's not the most intellectual job in the world, but I do have to know the letters.

~Vanna White

The trouble with unemployment is that the minute you wake up in the morning you're on the job.

~Slappy White

The trouble with retirement is that you never get a day off.

~Abe Lemons

The trouble with the rat race is that even if you win, you're still a rat.

~Lily Tomlin

Never wear a backwards baseball cap to an interview unless applying for the job of umpire.

~Dan Zevin

Oh, you hate your job? Why didn't you say so? There's a support group for that. It's called EVERYBODY, and they meet at the bar.

~Drew Carey

Rules to Live By

Never go to bed mad. Stay up and fight.
~Phyllis Diller

Если you're going to do something tonight that you'll be sorry
for tomorrow morning, sleep late.
~Henny Youngman

Don't worry about the world coming to an end today. It's
already tomorrow in Australia.
~Charles M. Schulz

Never go to a doctor whose house plants have died.
~Erma Bombeck

Always go to other people's funerals otherwise they won't come to yours.

~Yogi Berra

∽

Never take a cross country trip with a kid who has just learned to whistle.

~Jean Deuel

∽

Never raise your hands to your kids. It leaves your groin unprotected.

~Red Buttons

∽

If thine enemy offend thee, give his child a drum.

~Fran Lebowitz

∽

Love thy neighbor as thyself, but choose your neighborhood.

~Louise Beal

∽

Never answer an anonymous letter.

~Yogi Berra

∽

Never hold discussions with the monkey when the organ grinder is in the room.

~Winston Churchill

∾

When somebody tells you nothing is impossible, ask him to dribble a football.

~Author Unknown

∾

Never ask a barber if you need a haircut.

~Warren Buffett

∾

Never buy a portable television set from a man in the street who is out of breath.

~Arnold Glasow

∾

You can get more done with a kind word and a gun, than with a gun alone.

~Al Capone

∾

Always read something that will make you look good if you die in the middle of it.

~P.J. O'Rourke

∾

When life gives you lemons, squirt someone in the eye.

~Cathy Guisewite

∾

Never keep up with the Joneses. Drag them down to your level. It's cheaper.

~Quentin Crisp

∾

When your work speaks for itself, don't interrupt.

~Henry Kaiser

∾

Before you criticize someone, you should walk a mile in their shoes. That way, when you criticize them, you're a mile away and you have their shoes.

~Jack Handey

∾

Never fight an inanimate object.

~P.J. O'Rourke

∾

Never pick a fight with an ugly person, they've got nothing to lose.

~Robin Williams

∾

If two wrongs don't make a right, try three.

~Laurence J. Peter

∽

Never slap a man who's chewin' tobacco.

~Will Rogers

∽

Never stand between a dog and the hydrant.

~John Peters

∽

It is better to give than receive — especially advice.

~Mark Twain

∽

Never argue with a fool, onlookers may not be able
to tell the difference.

~Mark Twain

∽

Always forgive your enemies — nothing annoys them
so much.

~Oscar Wilde

∽

Get the facts first. You can distort them later.

~Mark Twain

∽

Don't sweat the petty things and don't pet the sweaty things

~George Carlin

∽

Never play leapfrog with a unicorn.

~Author Unknown

The Laugh's On Me

Those who can't laugh at themselves leave the job to others.

~Author Unknown

Ꙩ

The person who knows how to laugh at himself will never cease to be amused.

~Shirley MacLaine

Ꙩ

You grow up the day you have your first real laugh — at yourself.

~Ethel Barrymore

Ꙩ

Laughing at our mistakes can lengthen our own life. Laughing at someone else's can shorten it.

~Cullen Hightower

Ꙩ

I'm not offended by dumb blonde jokes because I know that I'm not dumb. I also know I'm not blonde.

~Dolly Parton

⌒

The man who says his wife can't take a joke, forgets that she took him.

~Oscar Wilde

⌒

Laughter is the shortest distance between two people

~Victor Borge

⌒

Laugh and the world laughs with you. Snore and you sleep alone.

~Anthony Burgess

⌒

Laughter is a tranquilizer with no side effects.

~Arnold Glasow

⌒

He who laughs last didn't get it.

~Helen Giangregorio

⌒

If you want to make God laugh, tell Him your plans.

~Yiddish Proverb

❦

Laughter is the best medicine, but in certain situations the Heimlich maneuver may be more appropriate."

~Author Unknown

❦

Laughter and tears are both responses to frustration and exhaustion. I myself prefer to laugh, since there is less cleaning to do afterward.

~Kurt Vonnegut

❦

If you want to make an audience laugh, you dress a man up like an old lady and push her down the stairs. If you want to make comedy writers laugh, you push an actual old lady down the stairs.

~Tina Fey

❦

Nothing can confound a wise man more than laughter from a dunce.

~Lord Byron

❦

An onion can make people cry, but there has never been a
vegetable invented to make them laugh.

~Will Rogers

಄

I am thankful for laughter, except when milk comes out
of my nose.

~Woody Allen

಄

But the fact that some geniuses were laughed at
does not imply that all who are laughed at are geniuses.
They laughed at Columbus, they laughed at Fulton,
they laughed at the Wright brothers. But they also laughed
at Bozo the Clown.

~Carl Sagan

಄

Instead of working for the survival of the fittest, we should
be working for the survival of the wittiest — then we can
all die laughing.

~Lily Tomlin

಄

I believe that laughter is a language of God and that we can all
live happily ever laughter.

~Yakov Smirnoff

಄

A pun is the lowest form of humor, unless you thought of it yourself.

~Doug Larson

❦

Hanging is too good for a man who makes puns; he should be drawn and quoted.

~Fred Allen

❦

Analyzing humor is like dissecting a frog. Few people are interested and the frog dies of it.

~E.B. White

❦

Tragedy is when I cut my finger. Comedy is when you fall into an open sewer and die.

~Mel Brooks

❦

What may seem depressing or even tragic to one person may seem like an absolute scream to another person, especially if he has had between four and seven beers.

~Dave Barry

❦

Imagination was given to man to compensate him for what he is not; a sense of humor to console him for what he is.

~*Francis Bacon*

∾

Everything is funny as long as it is happening to somebody else.

~*Will Rogers*

∾

That is the saving grace of humor, if you fail no one is laughing at you.

~*A. Whitney Brown*

∾

I think if I ever did actually laugh my ass off, I would get serious real fast.

~*Ed Smith*

Keep smiling — it makes people wonder what you've been up to.

~*Author Unknown*

It's Like

&

The human mind is like a TV set. When it goes blank,
it's a good idea to turn off the sound.

~Author Unknown

Stupidity is like nuclear power, it can be used for good or
evil. But you still don't want to get any on you.

~Scott Adams

Opinions are like feet. Everybody's got a couple, and
they usually stink.

~Jim Slattery

Trying to be a first-rate reporter on the average
American newspaper is like trying to play Bach's
"St. Matthew's Passion" on a ukulele.

~Ben Bagdikian

Writing about music is like dancing about architecture.

~Elvis Costello

∽

Balancing the budget is like going to heaven. Everybody wants to do it, but nobody wants to take the trip.

~Phil Gramm

∽

Praying is like a rocking chair — it'll give you something to do, but it won't get you anywhere.

~Gypsy Rose Lee

∽

Baseball is like church. Many attend, few understand.

~Leo Durocher

∽

Putting lights in Wrigley Field is like putting aluminum siding on the Sistine Chapel.

~Roger Simon

∽

Cricket is like the Middle East; the more you talk about it, the more confusing it gets

~Dan Denning

∽

Watching football is like watching pornography. There's plenty of action, and I can't take my eyes off it, but when it's over, I wonder why the hell I spent an afternoon doing it.

~Luke Salisbury

⁓

Sex is like snow, you never know how many inches you're going to get or how long it will last.

~Sophia Loren

⁓

Society, my dear, is like salt water, good to swim in but hard to swallow.

~Arthur Stringer

⁓

A program is like a nose — sometimes it runs, sometimes it blows.

~Howard Rose

⁓

Being in the army is like being in the Boy Scouts, except that the Boy Scouts have adult supervision.

~Blake Clark

Telling a teenager the facts of life is like giving a fish a bath.

~Arnold Glasow

⁓

Life is like a dogsled team. If you ain't the lead dog, the scenery never changes.

~Lewis Grizzard

∽

Life is like a sewer — what you get out of it depends on what you put into it.

~Tom Lehrer

∽

Life is like eating artichokes, you have got to go through so much to get so little.

~Thomas Aloysius Dorgan

∽

Resentment is like taking poison and waiting for the other person to die.

~Malachy McCourt

∽

It's a little like wrestling a gorilla. You don't quit when you're tired you quit when the gorilla is tired.

~Robert Strauss

∽

My game is like a cross between karaoke and rap: crap.

~Nick Faldo

∽

Asking a working writer what he thinks about critics is like asking a lamppost how it feels about dogs.

~*Christopher Hampton*

∽

Expecting the world to treat you fairly because you are good is like expecting the bull not to charge because you are a vegetarian.

~*Dennis Wholey*

∽

Marriage is like twirling a baton, turning hand springs or eating with chopsticks. It looks easy until you try it.

~*Helen Rowland*

∽

Alimony is like buying hay for a dead horse.

~*Groucho Marx*

∽

Husbands are like fires. They go out when unattended.

~*Zsa Zsa Gabor*

∽

You need this man in your life like a moose needs a hat rack.

~*Ann Landers*

∽

Men are like wine. Some turn to vinegar, but the best
improve with age

~Pope John XXIII

A woman is like a teabag. You can't tell how strong she is
until you put her in hot water.

~Nancy Reagan

Duct tape is like the Force. It has a light side, a dark
side, and it holds the universe together.

~Carl Zwanzig

Hearts On Fire

Nobody will ever win the battle of the sexes. There's too much fraternizing with the enemy.

~Henry Kissinger

If you love someone, set them free. If they come back, they're probably broke.

~Rhonda Dickson

There is nothing wrong with making love with the light on. Just make sure the car door is closed.

~George Burns

I had a rose named after me and I was very flattered. But I was not pleased to read the description in the catalog: "No good in a bed, but fine against a wall."

~Eleanor Roosevelt

The difference between sex and death is that with death you can do it alone and no one is going to make fun of you.

~Woody Allen

∽

There is a place you can touch a woman that will drive her crazy. Her heart.

~Melanie Griffith

∽

The fastest way to a man's heart is through his chest.

~Roseanne Barr

∽

The only time a woman really succeeds in changing a man is when he's a baby.

~Natalie Wood

∽

I know what men want. Men want to be really, really close to someone who will leave them alone.

~Elayne Boosler

∽

When I eventually met Mr. Right I had no idea that his first name was Always.

~Rita Rudner

∽

Men who have pierced ears are better prepared for marriage.
They've experienced pain and bought jewelry.

~Rita Rudner

❦

I always look for a woman who has a tattoo.
I see a woman with a tattoo, and I'm thinking, okay,
here's a gal who's capable of making a decision she'll regret
in the future.

~Richard Jeni

❦

When a girl says she wants to be friends with benefits,
I always ask if that includes dental insurance.

~Jarod Kintz

❦

A man on a date wonders if he'll get lucky. The woman
already knows.

~Monica Piper

❦

I was on a date with this really hot model. Well, it wasn't
really a date date. We just ate dinner and saw a movie.
Then the plane landed.

~Dave Attell

❦

It's the magnetic theory of dating. They attract each other because they repel everyone else.

~Malcolm Kushner

༄

I'm single by choice. Not my choice.

~Orny Adams

༄

My boyfriend and I broke up. He wanted to get married and I didn't want him to.

~Rita Rudner

༄

Marriage is a great institution, but I'm not ready for an institution.

~Mae West

༄

All men make mistakes, but married men find out about them sooner.

~Red Skelton

༄

Marriage is the triumph of imagination over intelligence. Second marriage is the triumph of hope over experience.

~Oscar Wilde

༄

I don't think I'll get married again. I'll just find a woman
I don't like and give her a house.

~*Lewis Grizzard*

∽

Why get married and make one man miserable when I can stay
single and make thousands miserable?

~*Carrie Snow*

∽

I've been in love with the same woman for forty-one years.
If my wife finds out, she'll kill me.

~*Henny Youngman*

∽

My husband and I divorced over religious differences. He
thought he was God, and I didn't.

~*Author Unknown*

∽

My husband said he needed more space. So I locked him
outside.

~*Roseanne Barr*

∽

Three things have helped me through the ordeals of life; an
understanding husband, a good analyst, and millions of dollars.

~*Mary Tyler Moore*

∽

Only two things are necessary to keep one's wife happy.
One is to let her think she is having her own way, and
the other is to let her have it.

~Lyndon B. Johnson

Adam and Eve had an ideal marriage. He didn't have to hear
about all the men she could have married, and she didn't
have to hear about the way his mother cooked.

~Kimberly Broyles

The four most important words in any marriage…
"I'll do the dishes."

~Author Unknown

Friends and Family

Friends are like bras: close to your heart and
there for support.

~Donna Roberts

Money can't buy friends, but you can get a better
class of enemy.

~Spike Milligan

The imaginary friends I had as a kid dropped me because
their friends thought I didn't exist.

~Aaron Machado

Outside of a dog, a book is man's best friend. Inside of a dog,
it's too dark to read.

~Groucho Marx

A true friend stabs you in the front.

~Oscar Wilde

∽

One good reason to only maintain a small circle of friends is that three out of four murders are committed by people who know the victim.

~George Carlin

∽

Families are like fudge — mostly sweet with a few nuts.

~Author Unknown

∽

Happiness is having a large, loving, caring, close-knit family in another city.

~George Burns

∽

The other night I ate at a real nice family restaurant. Every table had an argument going.

~George Carlin

∽

There is no such thing as fun for the whole family.

~Jerry Seinfeld

∽

Marry an orphan: you'll never have to spend boring holidays
with the in-laws.

~George Carlin

❧

I told my mother-in-law that my house was her house, and she
said, "Get the hell off my property."

~Joan Rivers

❧

I saw six men kicking and punching the mother-in-law.
My neighbour said "Are you going to help?" I said,
"No, six should be enough."

~Les Dawson

❧

I'm going home next week. It's kind of a family emergency.
My family is coming here.

~Rita Rudner

❧

You know, when you're little, your dad, you think he's
Superman. Then you grow up and realize he's just a guy
who wears a cape.

~Dave Attell

❧

I never got along with my dad. Kids used to come up to me and say, "My dad can beat up your dad." I'd say, "Yeah? When?"

~Bill Hicks

∽

When I was a boy, my mother wore a mood ring. When she was in a good mood it turned blue. In a bad mood, it left a big red mark on my forehead.

~Jeff Shaw

∽

My mother's menu consisted of two choices: Take it or leave it.

~Buddy Hackett

∽

My mother buried three husbands, and two of them were just napping.

~Rita Rudner

∽

I took my parents back to the airport today. They leave tomorrow.

~Margaret Smith

∽

Psychiatry enables us to correct our faults by confessing our parents' shortcomings.

~Laurence J. Peter

∽

My sister had a baby. I can't wait to find out if I'm an aunt or an uncle.

~Gracie Allen

∽

Insanity is hereditary — you get it from your children.

~Sam Levenson

∽

When my kids become wild and unruly, I use a nice, safe play-pen. When they're finished, I climb out.

~Erma Bombeck

∽

If your parents never had children, chances are you won't either.

~Dick Cavett

∽

A suburban mother's role is to deliver children; obstetrically once and by car forever after.

~Peter De Vries

∽

Never have more children than you have car windows.

~Erma Bombeck

∽

The best way to keep children at home is to make the home
atmosphere pleasant — and let the air out of their tires.

~Dorothy Parker

∽

If you want your children to listen, try talking softly —
to someone else.

~Ann Landers

∽

Ask your child what he wants for dinner only if he's buying.

~Fran Lebowitz

∽

Always be nice to your children because they are the ones who
will choose your rest home.

~Phyllis Diller

You Talking to Me?

The greatest danger in communication is the illusion it has been achieved.

~George Bernard Shaw

Never mistake legibility for communication.

~David Carson

The fact that no one understands you doesn't make you an artist.

~ Author Unknown

Two monologues do not make a dialogue.

~Jeff Daly

The opposite of talking isn't listening. The opposite of talking is waiting.

~Fran Lebowitz

One advantage of talking to yourself is that you know at least
somebody's listening.

~Franklin P. Jones

∽

I talk to myself a lot. That bothers some people because
I use a megaphone.

~Steven Wright

∽

They say that women talk too much. If you have worked
in Congress, you know that the filibuster was invented
by men.

~Clare Boothe Luce

∽

Women speak because they wish to speak, whereas
a man speaks only when driven to speech by something
outside himself — like, for instance, he can't find any
clean socks.

~Jean Kerr

∽

You never realize how the human voice can change until a
woman stops yelling at her husband and answers the phone.

~Neal O'Hara

∽

The telephone is a good way to talk to people without having to offer them a drink.

~Fran Lebowitz

∽

It is always the best policy to speak the truth — unless, of course, you are an exceptionally good liar.

~Jerome K. Jerome

∽

Speech is conveniently located midway between thought and action, where it often substitutes for both.

~John Andrew Holmes

∽

In America we can say what we think, and even if we can't think, we can say it anyhow.

~Charles Kettering

∽

It's so simple to be wise. Just think of something stupid to say and then don't say it.

~Sam Levenson

∽

Tis better to be silent and be thought a fool, than to speak and remove all doubt.

~Abraham Lincoln

∽

If there are no stupid questions, then what kind of questions do stupid people ask? Do they get smart just in time to ask questions?

~*Scott Adams*

∽

Many wise words are spoken in jest, but they don't compare with the number of stupid words spoken in earnest.

~*Sam Levenson*

∽

Nothing sways the stupid more than arguments they can't understand.

~*Cardinal De Retz*

∽

Nothing is as frustrating as arguing with someone who knows what he's talking about.

~*Sam Ewing*

∽

It takes a big man to admit when he's wrong, and an even bigger one to keep his mouth shut when he's right.

~*Jim Fiebig*

∽

People will accept your idea much more readily if you tell them Benjamin Franklin said it first.

~David H. Comins

∽

Never settle with words what you can accomplish with a flame thrower.

~Bruce Feirstein

∽

Man does not live by words alone, despite the fact that sometimes he has to eat them.

~Broderick Crawford

∽

I won't insult your intelligence by suggesting that you really believe what you just said.

~William F. Buckley Jr.

∽

I have never seen an ass who talked like a human being, but I have met many human beings who talked like asses.

~Heinrich Heine

∽

Man invented language to satisfy his deep need to complain.

~Lily Tomlin

∽

If the English language made any sense, lackadaisical would have something to do with a shortage of flowers.

~Doug Larson

After twelve years of therapy my psychiatrist said something that brought tears to my eyes. He said, "No hablo ingles."

~Ronnie Shakes

When I want your opinion, I'll remove the duct tape.

~ Author Unknown

They say you shouldn't say nothin' about the dead unless it's good. He's dead. Good!

~Moms Mabley

Defining Moments

The word aerobics comes from two Greek words: aero,
meaning "ability to," and bics, meaning "withstand
tremendous boredom."

~Dave Barry

Nouvelle Cuisine, roughly translated, means: I can't believe
I paid ninety-six dollars and I'm still hungry.

~Mike Kalin

A professor is someone who talks in someone else's sleep.

~W.H.Auden

A classic is something that everybody wants to have read and
nobody wants to read.

~Mark Twain

An encyclopedia is a system for collecting dust in
alphabetical order.

~*Mike Barfield*

∾

Opera is when a guy gets stabbed in the back and, instead of
bleeding, he sings.

~*Robert Benchley*

∾

Frisbeetarianism is the belief that when you die, your soul
goes up on the roof and gets stuck.

~*George Carlin*

∾

Good manners: The noise you don't make when
you're eating soup.

~*Bennett Cerf*

∾

"Normal" is just a setting on your dryer.

~*Patsy Clairmont*

∾

Baloney is just salami with an inferiority complex.

~*Ellen DeGeneres*

∾

A bargain is something you can't use at a price you can't resist.

~Franklin P. Jones

❧

A genius is a man who can rewrap a new shirt and not have any pins left over.

~Dino Levi

❧

An intellectual is a man who takes more words than necessary to tell more than he knows.

Dwight D. Eisenhower

❧

A critic is someone who never actually goes to the battle, yet who afterwards comes out shooting the wounded.

~Tyne Daly

❧

A diplomat is a man who always remembers a woman's birthday but never remembers her age.

~Robert Frost

❧

A statesman is any politician it's considered safe to name a school after.

~Bill Vaughn

❧

A gentleman is one who never hurts anyone's feelings unintentionally.

~Oscar Wilde

৵৩

Bigamy is having one wife too many. Monogamy is the same.

~Oscar Wilde

৵৩

To be positive is to be mistaken at the top of one's voice.

~Ambrose Bierce

৵৩

Channeling is just bad ventriloquism. You use another voice, but people can see your lips moving.

~Penn Jillette

৵৩

Foresight is knowing when to shut your mouth before someone suggests it.

~Author Unknown

৵৩

Tact is the art of making guests feel at home when that's really where you wish they were.

~George E. Bergman

৵৩

The power of accurate observation is often called cynicism
by those who have not got it.

~George Bernard Shaw

∽

We are not retreating — we are advancing in
another direction.

~General Douglas MacArthur

∽

We didn't lose the game; we just ran out of time.

~Vince Lombardi

∽

Don't think of it as failure. Think of it as
time-released success.

~Robert Orben

∽

I've never really thought of myself as depressed as much as
paralyzed by hope.

~Maria Bamford

∽

I'm not overweight. I'm just nine inches too short.

~Shelley Winters

∽

Creativity is allowing yourself to make mistakes. Art is knowing which ones to keep.

~Scott Adams

Skill is successfully walking a tightrope over Niagara Falls. Intelligence is not trying.

~Author Unknown

Excellent Observations

If you think you have someone eating out of your hand, it's a good idea to count your fingers.

~Martin Buxbaum

There's always free cheese in a mousetrap.

~Author Unknown

There's always free cheese in a mousetrap.

Every fight is a food fight when you're a cannibal.

~Demetri Martin

The trouble with eating Italian food is that five or six days later you're hungry again.

~George Miller

You're not drunk if you can lie on the floor without holding on.

~*Dean Martin*

❧

A word to the wise ain't necessary, it's the stupid ones who need advice.

~*Bill Cosby*

❧

The difference between genius and stupidity is that genius has its limits.

~*Albert Einstein*

❧

Think of how stupid the average person is, and realize half of them are stupider than that.

~*George Carlin*

❧

Anybody can win unless there happens to be a second entry.

~*George Ade*

❧

Glory is fleeting, but obscurity is forever.

~*Napoleon Bonaparte*

❧

If all else fails, immortality can always be assured by spectacular error.

~John Kenneth Galbraith

ה‍ص

Just because nobody complains doesn't mean that all parachutes are perfect.

~Benny Hill

ה‍ص

If no one ever took risks, Michelangelo would have painted the Sistine floor.

~Neil Simon

ה‍ص

Sometimes the road less traveled is less traveled for a reason.

~Jerry Seinfeld

ה‍ص

The man who says he is willing to meet you halfway is usually a poor judge of distance.

~Laurence J. Peter

ה‍ص

The trouble with being punctual is that nobody's there to appreciate it.

~Franklin P. Jones

ה‍ص

Doing nothing is very hard to do...you never know when you're finished.

~Leslie Nielsen

❦

If the minimum wasn't acceptable it wouldn't be called the minimum.

~George Muncaster

❦

If you want to say it with flowers, a single rose says: "I'm cheap!"

~Delta Burke

❦

When women are depressed they either eat or go shopping. Men invade another country.

~Elayne Boosler

❦

Football combines the two worst things about America: it is violence punctuated by committee meetings.

~George Will

❦

If you torture the data long enough it will confess to anything.

~John Thompson

❦

As long as there is algebra, there will be prayer in school.

~*Larry Miller*

Remember, anyone can juggle for a second.

~*John Alejandro King*

In the land of the skunks he who has half a nose is king.

~*Chris Farley*

You'll never catch a nudist with his pants down.

~*David Letterman*

It's easier to put on slippers than to carpet the whole world.

~*Al Franken*

The best car safety device is a rear-view mirror with a cop in it.

~*Dudley Moore*

There's a difference between a philosophy and a bumper sticker.

~*Charles M. Schulz*

A clear conscience is usually the sign of a bad memory.

~Steven Wright

A positive attitude may not solve all your problems, but it will annoy enough people to make it worth the effort.

~Herm Albright

We the People

⚮

Democracy means that anyone can grow up to be president,
and anyone who doesn't grow up can be vice president.

~Johnny Carson

The Vice Presidency is sort of like the last cookie
on the plate. Everybody insists he won't take it, but
somebody always does.

~Bill Vaughn

You don't have to fool all the people all of the time; you just
have to fool enough to get elected.

~Gerald Barzan

He knows nothing; and he thinks he knows everything. That
clearly points to a political career.

~George Bernard Shaw

Ninety percent of the politicians give the other ten percent a bad name.

~Henry Kissinger

∽

Sure there are dishonest men in local government. But there are dishonest men in national government too.

~Richard Nixon

∽

Being in politics is like being a football coach. You have to be smart enough to understand the game, and dumb enough to think it's important.

~Eugene McCarthy

∽

The word "politics" is derived from the word "poly" meaning "many", and the word "ticks" meaning "blood sucking parasites."

~Larry Hardiman

∽

Politicians are people who, when they see the light at the end of the tunnel, order more tunnel.

~John Quinton

∽

A politician is a man who will double cross that bridge
when he comes to it.

~Oscar Levant

‿

You said in your book that at the end of the day, every
politician is human. What about during the day?

~Stephen Colbert

‿

The difference between politics and baseball is that in baseball,
when you get caught stealing, you're out.

~Ron Dentinger

‿

My definition of a redundancy is an air-bag in a
politician's car.

~Larry Hagman

‿

The reason there are two senators for each state is so
that one can be the designated driver.

~Jay Leno

‿

Under capitalism, man exploits man. Under communism,
it's just the opposite.

~John Kenneth Galbraith

‿

You don't have to spend much time in Washington to
appreciate the prophetic vision of the man who
designed all the streets there. They go in circles.

~Ronald Reagan

∽

Where but in Washington would they call the department
that's in charge of everything outdoors, everything
outside, the Department of Interior.

~Ronald Reagan

∽

In my many years I have come to a conclusion that one
useless man is a shame, two is a law firm, and three
or more is a congress.

~John Adams

∽

With Congress, every time they make a joke it's a law; and
every time they make a law it's a joke.

~Will Rogers

∽

Congress is so strange. A man gets up to speak and says
nothing. Nobody listens — and then everybody disagrees.

~Boris Marshalov

∽

I have wondered at times what the Ten Commandments
would have looked like if Moses had run them
through the U.S. Congress.

~Ronald Reagan

∽

The difference between death and taxes is death doesn't get
worse every time Congress meets.

~Will Rogers

∽

Congressmen are so damned dumb, they could throw
themselves on the ground and miss.

~James Traficant

∽

I have learned the difference between a cactus and a caucus.
On a cactus, the pricks are on the outside.

~Mo Udall

∽

Assuming either the Left Wing or the Right Wing gained
control of the country, it would probably fly around
in circles.

~Pat Paulsen

∽

Feeling good about government is like looking on the bright side of any catastrophe. When you quit looking on the bright side, the catastrophe is still there.

~P.J. O'Rourke

Relying on the government to protect your privacy is like asking a peeping tom to install your window blinds.

~John Perry Barlow

The government is like a baby's alimentary canal, with a happy appetite at one end and no responsibility at the other.

~Ronald Reagan

I like space. The higher you go, the smaller the federal government looks.

~Ronald Reagan

Taxation with representation ain't so hot either.

~Gerald Barzan

As the Years Go By

Age is an issue of mind over matter. If you don't mind, it doesn't matter.

~Mark Twain

Age doesn't matter, unless you're a cheese.

~Billie Burke

The secret of staying young is to live honestly, eat slowly, and lie about your age.

~Lucille Ball

My doctor recently told me that jogging could add years to my life. I think he was right. I feel ten years older already.

~Milton Berle

You know you're getting old when you stoop to tie your
shoelaces and wonder what else you could do while
you're down there.

~George Burns

∾

One trouble with growing older is that it gets progressively
tougher to find a famous historical figure who didn't
amount to much when he was your age.

~Bill Vaughn

∾

You know you're getting old when the candles cost more
than the cake.

~Bob Hope

∾

He has a profound respect for old age. Especially when
it's bottled.

~Gene Fowler

∾

Don't worry about avoiding temptation...as you grow older,
it will avoid you.

~Winston Churchill

∾

By the time a man is wise enough to watch his step, he's too old to go anywhere.

~Billy Crystal

∾

Wisdom doesn't necessarily come with age. Sometimes age just shows up all by itself.

~Tom Wilson

∾

The surprising thing about young fools is how many survive to become old fools.

~Doug Larson

∾

No one is ever old enough to know better.

~Holbrook Johnson

∾

Some people might say, "Who would want to be 90?" And I say, "Anyone who is 89."

~Phyllis Diller

∾

If you live to the age of a hundred you have it made because very few people die past the age of a hundred.

~George Burns

∾

The years between fifty and seventy are the hardest.
You are always being asked to do things, and yet you
are not decrepit enough to turn them down.

~T. S. Eliot

೧൭

Looking fifty is great — if you're sixty.

~Joan Rivers

೧൭

Middle age is when your classmates are so gray and wrinkled
and bald they don't recognize you.

~Bennett Cerf

೧൭

I was born in 1962. True. And the room next to me
was 1963.

~Joan Rivers

೧൭

At my age getting a second doctor's opinion is kinda like
switching slot machines.

~Jimmy Carter

೧൭

I'm at an age when my back goes out more than I do.

~Phyllis Diller

೧൭

The first sign of maturity is the discovery that the volume knob also turns to the left.

~Jerry M. Wright

❧

Very few people do anything creative after the age of thirty-five. The reason is that very few people do anything creative before the age of thirty-five.

~Joel Hildebrand

❧

There are three ages of man — youth, middle age, and "you're looking wonderful."

~Cardinal Francis Spellman

❧

I've found the secret of youth: I lie about my age.

~Bob Hope

❧

The secret of eternal youth is arrested development.

~Alice Roosevelt Longworth

❧

We could certainly slow the aging process down if it had to work its way through Congress.

~Will Rogers

❧

We are young only once, after that we need some
other excuse.

~Author Unknown

∾

You can only be young once. But you can always
be immature.

~Dave Barry

∾

I believe in loyalty. When a woman reaches an age she likes, she
should stick with it.

~Eva Gabor

∾

You're never too old to become younger.

~Mae West

❧

Appendices

Appendix: Favorite Funny Quotes

Quote:_____

_____

_____

Quote:_____

_____

_____

Quote:_____

_____

_____

Quote:_____

_____

_____

Quote:_____

_____

_____

Quote:_____

_____

_____

Appendix: Humor Checklist

Advertising
I find it funny that…

_____

_____

_____

_____

_____

_____

_____

_____

_____

_____

_____

_____

_____

_____

_____

_____

_____

_____

Celebrities

I find it funny that…

_____

_____

_____

_____

_____

_____

_____

_____

_____

_____

_____

Family

I find it funny that…

_____

_____

_____

_____

_____

_____

_____

_____

_____

_____

Health
I find it funny that...

_____

_____

_____

_____

_____

_____

_____

_____

_____

_____

In the News
I find it funny that...

_____

_____

_____

_____

_____

_____

_____

_____

_____

_____

Neighborhood
I find it funny that…

_____

_____

_____

_____

_____

_____

_____

_____

_____

_____

_____

Politics
I find it funny that…

_____

_____

_____

_____

_____

_____

_____

_____

_____

_____

_____

Sports
I find it funny that...

_____

_____

_____

_____

_____

_____

_____

_____

_____

_____

_____

Technology
I find it funny that...

_____

_____

_____

_____

_____

_____

_____

_____

_____

_____

_____

Travel

I find it funny that…

_____

_____

_____

_____

_____

_____

_____

_____

_____

_____

Work

I find it funny that…

_____

_____

_____

_____

_____

_____

_____

_____

_____

_____

Other
I find it funny that …

_____

_____

_____

_____

_____

_____

_____

_____

_____

_____

Other
I find it funny that …

_____

_____

_____

_____

_____

_____

_____

_____

_____

_____

Other

I find it funny that ...

_____

_____

_____

_____

_____

_____

_____

_____

_____

_____

_____

Appendix: Humor Journal

Things you found funny in…

January:_____

_____

_____

_____

_____

_____

_____

_____

February:_____

_____

_____

_____

_____

_____

_____

_____

March:_____

_____

_____

_____

_____

_____

_____

_____

_____

April:_____

_____

_____

_____

_____

_____

_____

_____

_____

May:_____

_____

_____

_____

_____

_____

_____

_____

_____

June:_____
_____
_____
_____
_____
_____
_____
_____
_____
_____

July:_____
_____
_____
_____
_____
_____
_____
_____
_____
_____

August:_____
_____
_____
_____
_____
_____
_____
_____
_____

September:_____

_____
_____
_____
_____
_____
_____
_____
_____
_____
_____

October:_____

_____
_____
_____
_____
_____
_____
_____
_____
_____
_____

November:_____

_____
_____
_____
_____
_____
_____
_____
_____
_____
_____

December:_____

_____

_____

_____

_____

_____

_____

_____

_____

_____

Biographical Index

Adams, Jack: 1895-1968, Canadian hockey player
Adams, John: 1735-1826 2nd President of the United States
Adams, Orny: American comedian
Adams, Scott: 1957-   , American cartoonist
Ade, George: 1866-1944, American writer
Albright, Herm: 1876-1944, German-born painter and lithographer
Allen, Fred: 1894-1956, American comedian
Allen, Gracie: 1895-1964, American comedian
Allen, Woody: 1935-   , American comedian, director and writer
Attell, Dave: 1965-   , American comedian
Auden, W.H.: 1907-1973, Anglo-American poet
Averre, Berton: 1953-   , American musician

Bacon, Francis: 1561-1626, English philosopher
Bagdikian, Ben: 1920-   , American journalist
Bailey, Bernard: 1964-   , English comedian
Ball, Lucille: 1911-1989, American comedian
Bamford, Maria: 1970-   , American comedian
Barlow, John Perry: 1947-   , American poet and essayist
Barr, Roseanne: 1952-   , American comedian
Barry, Dave: 1947-   , American humorist
Barrymore, Ethel: 1879-1959, American actress
Benchley, Robert: 1889-1945, American humorist
Bergen, Edgar: 1903-1978, American ventriloquist

Berle, Milton: 1908-2002, American comedian
Bernhard, Sandra: 1955- , American comedian
Berra, Yogi: 1925- , American baseball player and manager
Bierce, Ambrose: 1842-1913, American journalist
Bombeck, Erma: 1927-1996, American humorist
Bonaparte, Napoleon: 1769-1821, Emperor of France
Boosler, Elayne: 1952- , American comedian
Borge, Victor: 1909-2000, Danish comedian and musician
Brooks, Mel: 1926- , American comedian, director, and writer
Brown, A. Whitney: 1952- , American comedian
Brown, Rita Mae: 1944- , American writer
Buckley Jr., William F.: 1925-2008, American writer
Buffett, Warren: 1930- , American investor
Burgess, Anthony: 1917-1993, English author
Burke, Billie: 1884-1970, American actress
Burke, Delta: 1956- , American actress
Burns, George: 1896-1996, American comedian
Buttons, Red: 1919-2006, American comedian
Buxbaum, Martin: 1912-1991, American writer
Byron, Lord: 1788-1824, English poet

Capone, Al: 1899-1947, American gangster
Carey, Drew: 1958- , American comedian
Carlin, George: 1937-2008, American comedian
Carson, David: 1952- , American graphic designer
Carson, Johnny: 1925-2005, American comedian and television host
Carter, Jimmy: 1924- , 39th President of the United States
Cavett, Dick: 1936- , American comedian and television host
Cerf, Bennett: 1898-1971, American publisher
Churchill, Winston: 1874-1965, British Prime Minister
Clark, Blake: 1946- , American actor
Colbert, Stephen: 1964- , American comedian
Collier, William: 1902-1987, American actor

Cosby, Bill: 1937-   , American comedian
Costello, Elvis: 1954-   , English musician
Crawford, Broderick: 1911-1986, American actor
Crisp, Quentin: 1908-1999, English writer
Crystal, Billy: 1948-   , American comedian

Daly, Tyne: 1946-   , American actress
Dawson, Les: 1931-1993, English comedian
DeGeneres, Ellen: 1958-   , American comedian
De Retz, Cardinal: 1613-1679, French churchman
De Vries, Peter: 1910-1993, American writer
Diller, Phyllis: 1917-2012, American comedian
Dorgan, Thomas Aloysius: 1877- 1929, American cartoonist
Drucker, Peter: 1909-2005, American writer and management consultant
Durocher, Leo: 1905-1991, American baseball player and manager

Einstein, Albert: 1879-1955, German-Swiss scientist
Eisenhower, Dwight D.: 1890-1969, 34th President of the United States
Eliot, T. S.: 1888-1965, American-born English poet
Ewing, Sam: 1949-   , American baseball player

Faldo, Nick: 1957-   , English golfer
Farley, Chris: 1964-1997, American comedian
Feirstein, Bruce: 1956-   , American humorist
Fey, Tina: 1970-   , American comedian and writer
Forbes, Malcolm: 1919-1990, American publisher
Fowler, Gene: 1890-1960, American writer
Foxworthy, Jeff: 1958-   , American comedian
Franken, Al: 1951-   , American comedian and senator
Frost, Robert: 1874-1963, American poet

Gabor, Eva: 1919-1995, Hungarian-born American actress
Gabor, Zsa Zsa: 1917- , Hungarian-born American actress
Galbraith, John Kenneth: 1908-2006, Canadian-American economist
Gallagher: 1946- , American comedian
Gavin, General John: 1929- , American general
Gramm, Phil: 1942- , American senator
Griffith, Melanie: 1957- , American actress
Grizzard, Lewis: 1946-1994, American humorist
Guisewite, Cathy: 1950- , American cartoonist

Hackett, Buddy: 1924-2003, American comedian
Hagman, Larry: 1931- , American actor
Hampton, Christopher: 1946- , British playwright
Handey, Jack: 1949- , American humorist
Hedberg, Mitch: 1968-2005, American comedian
Heine, Heinrich: 1797-1856, German poet
Hicks, Bill: 1961-1994, American comedian
Hightower, Cullen: 1923- , American writer
Hildebrand, Joel: 1881-1983, American chemistry professor
Hill, Benny: 1924-1992, English comedian
Holloway, Ian: 1963- , English soccer manager and player
Hope, Bob: 1903- 2003, American comedian
Hubbard, Kin: 1868-1930, American humorist

Jeni, Richard 1957-2007, American comedian
Jerome, Jerome K.: 1859-1927, English humorist
Jillette, Penn: 1955- , American magician and comedian
Johnson, Lyndon B.: 1908-1973, 36th President of the United States
Jones, Franklin P.: 1908-1980, American journalist

Kahn, Alice: 1943- , American writer
Kaiser, Henry: 1882-1967, American industrialist

Kerr, Jean: 1922-2003, American author and playwright
Kettering, Charles: 1876-1958, American inventor
King, John Alejandro: 1958-   , American CIA officer and humorist
Kintz, Jarod: 1982-   , American writer
Kissinger, Henry: 1923-   , German-born American Secretary of State
Kushner, Malcolm: 1952-   , American humor consultant

Lamb, Charles: 1775-1834, English critic
Landers, Ann: 1918- 2002, American journalist
Larson, Doug: 1926-   , American journalist
Lebowitz, Fran: 1950-   , American writer
Lec, Stanislaw J.: 1909-1966, Polish poet and aphorist
Lee, Gypsy Rose: 1911-1970, American entertainer
Lehrer, Tom: 1928-   , American musician and satirist
Lemons, Abe: 1922-2002, American basketball coach
Leno, Jay: 1950-   , American comedian
Letterman, David: 1947-   , American comedian
Levant, Oscar: 1906-1972, American musician and wit
Levenson, Sam: 1911- 1980, American humorist
Liebman, Wendy: 1961-   , American comedian
Lincoln, Abraham: 1809-1865, 16th President of the United States
Lombardi, Vince: 1913-1970, Italian-American football coach
Longworth, Alice Roosevelt: 1884-1980, American writer
Loren, Sophia: 1934-   , Italian actress
Luce, Clare Boothe: 1903-1987, American writer

Mabley, Moms: 1894-1975, American comedian
MacArthur, General Douglas: 1880-1964, American general
MacLaine, Shirley: 1934-   , American actress
Marquis, Don: 1878-1937, American humorist
Marshalov, Boris: 1898-1967, Russian writer

Martin, Dean: 1917-1995, American singer
Martin, Demetri: 1973- , American comedian
Martin, Steve: 1945- , American comedian
Marx, Groucho: 1890-1977, American comedian
McCarthy, Eugene: 1916-2005, American senator
McCourt, Malachy: 1931- , Irish-American actor
McDonald, Claude: 1925- , American writer
Miller, Dennis: 1953- , American comedian
Miller, George: 1950-2003, Australian comedian
Milligan, Spike: 1918-2002, British comedian
Moore, Dudley: 1935-2002, English actor
Moore, Mary Tyler: 1936- , American actress

Nielsen, Leslie: 1926-2010, Canadian-American actor
Nixon, Richard M.: 1913-1994, 37th President of the United States

O'Rourke, P.J.: 1947- , American writer
Orben, Robert: 1927- , American comedy writer

Parker, Dorothy: 1893-1967, American poet and wit
Parton, Dolly: 1946- , American singer
Paulsen, Pat: 1927-1997, American comedian
Peter, Laurence J.: 1919-1990, Canadian-born American educator
Pope John XXIII: 1881-1963, 261st Pope of the Catholic Church

Reagan, Nancy: 1921- , American actress and First Lady of the United States
Reagan, Ronald: 1911-2004, 40th President of the United States
Rivers, Joan: 1933-2014, American comedian
Rogers, Will: 1879-1935, American humorist
Roosevelt, Eleanor: 1884-1962, First Lady of the United States
Rowland, Helen: 1875-1950, American journalist and humorist.
Rudner, Rita: 1953- , American comedian
Russell, Bertrand: 1872-1970, British philosopher

Sagan, Carl: 1934-1996, American scientist
Salisbury, Luke: 1947-   , American writer
Schulz, Charles M.: 1922- 2000, American cartoonist
Seinfeld, Jerry: 1954-   , American comedian
Shaw, George Bernard: 1856-1950, Irish playwright
Simon, Neil: 1927-   , American playwright
Skelton, Red: 1913-1997, American comedian
Slattery, Jim: 1948-   , American politician
Smirnoff, Yakov: 1951-   , Ukrainian-born American comedian
Smothers, Tommy: 1937-   , American comedian
Spellman, Cardinal Francis: 1889-1967, American Archbishop of
New York
Stengel, Casey: 1890-1975, American baseball player and manager
Stilwell, Joseph: 1883-1946, American general
Strauss, Robert: 1983-   , American wrestler
Stringer, Arthur: 1874-1950, Canadian writer

Tomlin, Lily: 1939-   , American comedian
Townsend, Robert: 1920-1998, American business executive and
author
Traficant, James: 1941-   , American congressman
Twain, Mark: 1835-1910, American writer and humorist

Udall, Mo: 1922-1998, American congressman

Vaughn, Bill: 1915-1977, American writer
Vonnegut, Kurt: 1922-2007, American writer

West, Mae: 1893-1980, American actress
White, E.B.: 1899-1985, American writer
White, Slappy: 1921- 1995, American comedian
White, Vanna: 1957-   , American television personality
Wholey, Dennis: 1939-   , American television host
Wilde, Oscar: 1854-1900, Irish writer

Will, George: 1941-   , American journalist
Williams, Robin: 1951-2014, American comedian
Wilson, Tom: 1959-   , American comedian
Winters, Shelley: 1920-2006, American actress
Wood, Natalie: 1938-1981, American actress
Wright, Steven: 1955-   , American comedian

Youngman, Henny: 1906-1998, American comedian

Biographical Index

Malcolm Kushner, "America's Favorite Humor Consultant," is an internationally acclaimed expert on humor and communication. He is the author of *The Light Touch: How to Use Humor for Business Success, Public Speaking For Dummies, Vintage Humor for Wine Lovers* and *The Official Book of Mob Humor.* He is also the co-creator of a humor exhibit that appeared at the Ronald Reagan Presidential Library.

Kushner has been profiled in *Time Magazine, USA Today, The New York Times* and *The Washington Post.* His television and radio appearances include CNN, C-SPAN, Fox & Friends, National Public Radio, CNBC, "Voice of America" and "The Larry King Show." *The Wall Street Journal* has called him "irrepressible."

A popular speaker at corporate and association meetings, Kushner has keynoted everywhere from The Smithsonian Institution to the Inc. 500 Conference.

Visit his websites at:
www.kushnergroup.com
www.museumofhumor.com

He can be reached at
mk@kushnergroup.com

Malcolm Kushner & Associates

21400963R00080

Made in the USA
San Bernardino, CA
19 May 2015